THE COMPLETE BOOK OF HORSES

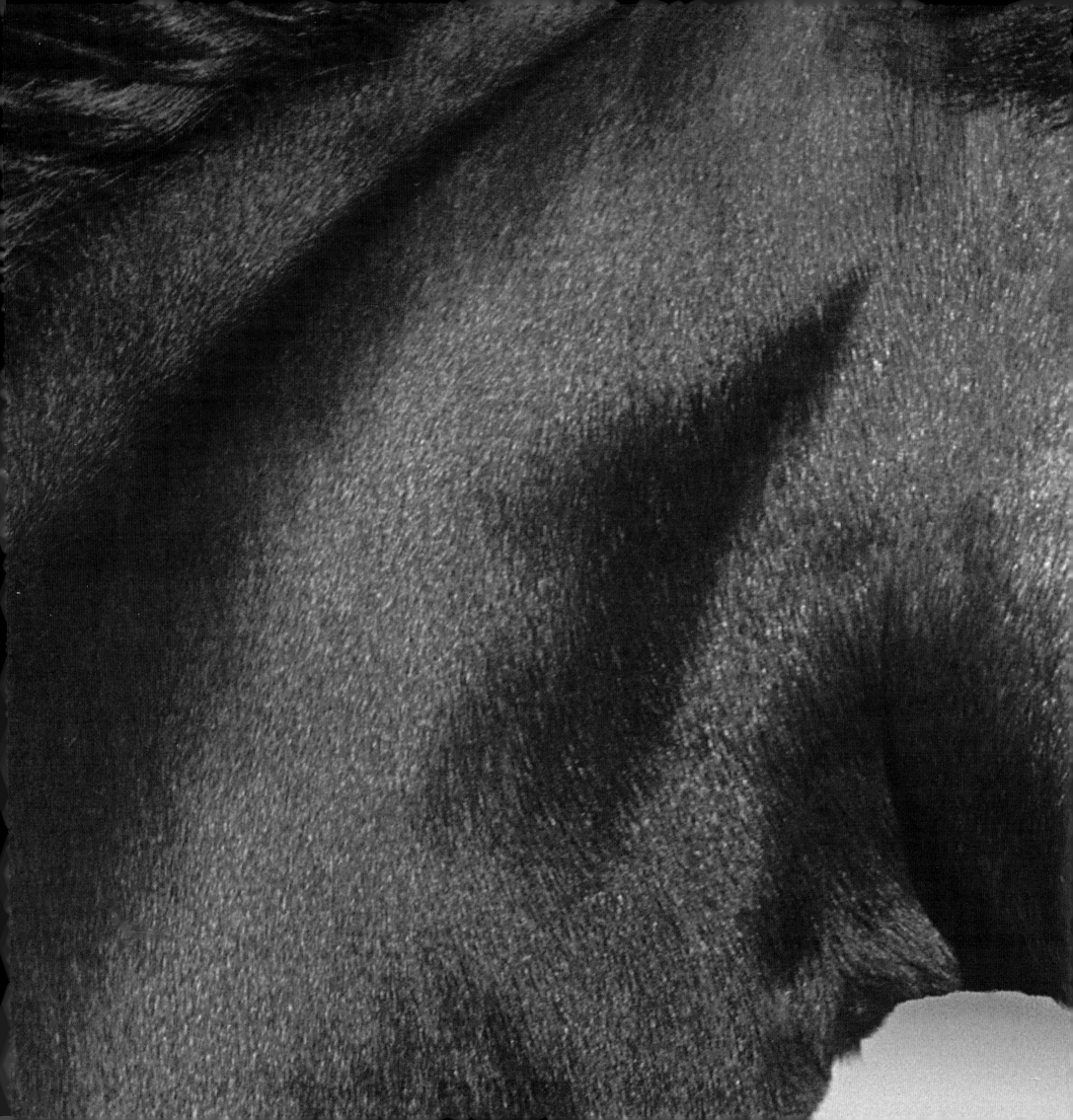

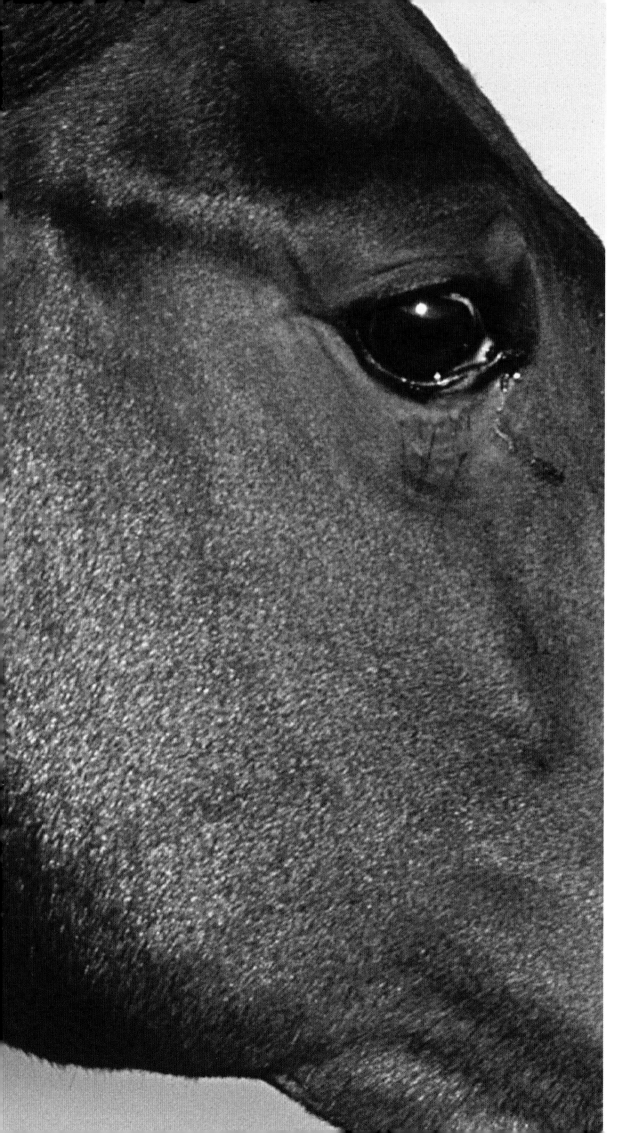

THE COMPLETE
BOOK OF HORSES

NICOLA JANE
SWINNEY

Kandour Ltd

Published by
Kandour Ltd
1-3 Colebrooke Place
London
N1 8HZ
UNITED KINGDOM

This edition printed in 2006
for Bookmart Ltd
Registered Number 2372865
Trading as Bookmart Ltd
Blaby Road
Wigston
Leicester LE18 4SE

First published 2006

10 9 8 7 6 5 4 3 2 1

Author: Nicola Jane Swinney
Editor: Tammy Seto
Design and Layout: Alexander Rose Publishing Limited
Photography Supplied by: Bob Langrish
Production: Karen Lomax

Printed and bound in China

ISBN-10: 1-904756-84-0

ISBN-13: 978-1-904756-84-2

Contents

ARABIANS
&
THOROUGHBREDS

Arabians & Thoroughbreds

A powerhouse of bone, sinew, and muscle, the modern Thoroughbred can gallop at speeds of up to forty-five miles per hour and can jump a distance of some thirty feet.

This equine athlete takes his name from the Arabic word "keheilan", which means pure blood — and more than ninety percent of modern Thoroughbreds can be traced back to just three stallions, all of which were Arabians.

Those stallions are the Byerly Turk, the Godolphin Arabian and the Darley Arabian. It has been suggested that the Byerly Turk was an Akhal-Teke — the desert's golden son — rather than an Arabian, but without doubt these are the most ancient and therefore purest of all equine breeds.

Surefooted, hardy, and independent, the original Arabian was held in high regard by his nomadic masters — indeed, the seventh century Prophet Mohammad boosted the horse's value by stating "No evil spirit shall dare enter a tent where there is a pure-bred horse". The Bedouins took this literally, and slept with their equines under the same canvas roof. And so began the timeless partnership between horse and man.

The Arab is a horse of great beauty, every little girl's fairy tale come true. But while he is maligned by some as a mere flashy "show pony", his influence on today's equines is unparalleled.

According to the Prophet Mohammed, the Arab was created by "condensing the wind". His creator is said to have proclaimed: "I have hung happiness from your forlock which hangs between your eyes; you shall be the Lord of the other animals. Men will follow you wherever you go; you shall be as good for pursuit as for flight; riches shall be on your back, and fortune shall come through your mediation."

Arabians & Thoroughbreds

Riches indeed. The Arab and his direct descendant, the Thoroughbred, command huge prices and there is a billion-dollar industry resting on the latter's back.

The Arabian blood was closely guarded by the Bedouin tribes, who fought constantly to keep him "Asil" (pure). The nomads treasured their horses, with whom they shared food, water, and shelter, and not just for their beauty. To the nomad, the horse represented wealth, and honour. The Arabian's stamina and turn of foot was invaluable when it came to raiding enemy tribes — raids that would reap riches such as goats, sheep, and camels to add to the raider's wealth and, more importantly to these proud people, status. It was usually the Arab mares used in these lightning attacks, as they were less likely to whicker to the enemy's horses and thus give away their presence.

These mares were priced beyond rubies to their Arabian masters, and were named for the sheikhs that owned them and bred from them. In time, five different lines were produced — Abeyan, Hadban, Hamdawi, Kehilan, and Seglawi — with distinctive attributes, which can still be seen in the modern Arab.

And he is a horse of undeniable beauty. He is unique among equines in that he has seventeen ribs, five lumbar vertebra, and sixteen tail bones; all other breeds have eighteen ribs, six lumbar vertebrae, and eighteen tail bones. His fine concave profile is accentuated by another unique feature, a shield-shaped bulge between his liquid eyes called the "jibbah", offset by small, curved ears. His head tapers to a small, neat muzzle that should fit into a half-cupped human hand. His arching neck joins his head at a point known as the "mitbah", an angle that gives his head great mobility and able to turn freely in any direction.

Arabians & Thoroughbreds

Apart from palomino, the Arabian is found in all solid colors. His desert ancestors were rarely black, because their masters believed it a bad color that absorbed heat, but it is found today and, along with the more common gray, adds to his exotic glory.

His comparatively short back and slender legs allow him to moved swiftly and with great elevation — the Arabian's floating trot is supremely comfortable as well as a joy to watch. He is popular as an endurance horse, because he has both speed and stamina, but it was the former that was to form the basis for a billion-dollar worldwide industry.

Not for nothing is horseracing in England called the "Sport of Kings". Richard the Lionheart (King Richard I) was said to have established racing on Epsom Moor, personally putting up the prizes, before King James I established the racetrack at Newmarket in Cambridge — now British horseracing's "HQ" — in the seventeenth century.

The existing native stock, probably Galloway ponies mixed with some Irish Hobby — a forerunner to the Connemara pony, Spanish, Neopolitan, and Barb blood. But these native running horses lacked speed and refinement. When the three desert horses — named, as was the custom of the day, after their respective owners, Thomas Darley, Lord Godolphin and Captain Robert Byerley — were brought to England from the Mediterranean Middle East in the late 1700s, they were to change the face of horseracing forever.

Certainly, the first two were Arabians. The Byerly Turk, taken from a captured Turkish officer by Capt Byerley (the second "E" was dropped because of a typographical error) in the siege of Buda in Hungary in 1688, is thought by some to have been an Akhal-Teke, although he

Arabians & Thoroughbreds

was reportedly of distinctly Arabian appearance. He served as the captain's charger in later campaigns, before standing at stud first in County Durham in the north of England, then at Goldsborough Hall in Yorkshire, where it is thought his remains were buried. He was dark brown with no white upon him and was prepotent, throwing dark brown, or black stock.

His great-great-grandson Herod was to establish the importance of the Byerly line, largely through his ancestor Diomed, winner of the first Epsom Derby in 1780. Diomed was exported to America, where he founded an equine dynasty.

The Darley Arabian was bought by Thomas Darley in Aleppo in Syria, and although it has been suggested he was a Syrian or Turkish breed, the accepted wisdom is that he was pure Arabian. A bay with a wide white blaze, and three white feet, the Darley Arabian sired Flying Childers — thought to be

the fastest racehorse ever and known affectionately as "Mile a Minute Childers" — and Whistlejacket, famously painted by Sir George Stubbs. Flying Childers' full-brother, Bartlet's Childers, was the great-grandsire of Eclipse, who was unbeaten in all of his eighteen races.

Perhaps the most romantic story of all three founding stallions is that of the Godolphin Arabian, who, legend has it, was found pulling a water cart in Paris. He was imported to England by Edward Coke in 1729, who subsequently used him to cover his own mare, Roxana. Another — probably apocryphal — account is that the Godolphin Arabian fought another stallion, called Hobgoblin, for Roxana, and won. The resulting colt, named Lath, was said to be a "very elegant and beautiful" horse, but his full-brother, Cade — sadly, the mare Roxana died after foaling him — although inferior on the racetrack, was to have far greater influence as a stallion

Arabians & Thoroughbreds

Edward Coke died in 1733, at the age of 32, and left some of his mares and foals — including Roxana and Lath — to his friend Francis, the second Earl of Godolphin. The rest of his horses he left to another friend, Roger Williams, from whom the Earl later purchased the Arabian.

Cade's most important son was Matchem — an adage of the day was "Snap for speed, and Matchem for truth and daylight". Snap was a grandson of Flying Childers, and passed on the line's precocious speed; Matchem provided equally desirably traits in racehorses — gameness and soundness. In all, Matchem was to sire 354 winners, stamping them all with excellent temperament and durability.

The first Thoroughbred to be imported in America was the Darley Arabian son, Bulle Rock, in 1730. He was 21 years old when he arrived, having raced successfully in England.

By 1800 more than 300 other Thoroughbreds were imported to the USA, among them the influential Messenger, who was to sire a highly successful line. His great-grandson, known as Rysdyk's Hambletonian, was the foundation sire of the American Standardbred.

Today, the American racing industry is worth almost $2 billion, with Kentucky at its heart. At the Keeneland Sales, racing's future stars exchange hands for record sums and, ironically, agents from England - the Thoroughbred's spiritual home - flock across "The Pond" on six-figure shopping trips.

While there is no doubting the Arabian's antiquity, there are those who believe the Akhal-Teke, his desert cousin, may be even older. This glorious golden equine takes his name from the Turkmenian tribe, Teke, that inhabited the Akhal oasis in the Kara Kum Desert in Turkmenia. Although

Arabians & Thoroughbreds

Russia claims him as her native breed, the Akhal-Teke actually predates the Soviet Union by thousands of years; excavations in southern Turkmenistan have uncovered skeletal remains of tall, fine-boned horses dating back to 2400 BC. Historic figures including Alexander the Great, Gengis Khan, and Marco Polo were devotees.

Like the Arabian and Thoroughbred, the Akhal-Teke is hot-blooded, and thus superbly adapted for a desert environment, able to withstand extreme heat, dry cold, and drought. When Russia annexed Turkmenistan some 500 years ago, she called the region's horses Argamak —a Turkic word meaning tall and refined. The first Akhal-Teke stud was founded by Russia at Zakaspiisky, near Ashkhabad, the capital of Turkmenistan. Only the best breeding stock were used at this stud, including the stallion Boinou, progenitor of the dominant Akhal-Teke lines still in use today.

Words such as lean, dry, refined epitomise the breed, as does his distinctive glowing metallic sheen, overlaying the basic coat color. Legend has it that when an Akhal-Teke was presented as a state gift to England's Queen Elizabeth II in 1956, the royal grooms spent some time trying to wash off what they thought was an unusual polish on the horse's coat.

IBERIAN

Iberian

Nobility is a word that might have been coined for the magnificent horses of the Iberian Peninsula. Their's is a story of life imitating art; the stuff of legend, and the diligence of man in recognizing and retaining a glorious heritage.

It is thought that the legend of the Centaur, the mythical half-man half-horse, arose from the oneness the Iberian warriors had with their equines, so together, so in harmony, they appeared as one creature.

Author Arsenio Raposa Cordeiro says in his book Cavalo Lusitano, o Filho do Vento (Lusitano Horse, Son of the Wind): "The perfect bond between Iberian man and horse may have provided the original inspiration behind the legend of the Centaur, a hybrid man-horse creature deemed to spring from the valleys of the Tagus River [in what is now Portugal].

"It was also believed that the mares of this region were sired by the wind, which accounted for the amazing speed with which they endowed their progeny."

The renowned Greek cavalry officer Xenophon — widely credited with the development of classical equitation, the foundation for modern horsemanship — eulogized the Iberian horse for his flamboyant, high-stepping action, great courage, and natural agility.

Homer mentions the horses of Iberia in The Iliad, written around 1,100BC, but it is thought that these equines go back far beyond that — cave paintings in the Iberian Peninsula of southern Spain date back to 20,000 or even 30,000BC.

Certainly, the horses of Iberia — the Andalusian, Lusitano, Alter-Real and the unprepossessing Sorraia — are of great antiquity, and have had almost as

Iberian

much influence on the world's equine breeds as the Arabian.

As volatile as the region of his birth, the Iberian horse was sculpted over the centuries by the various peoples, their cultures, and equines that occupied southern Spain throughout her long history. French, North African, Roman, German, and Moorish tribes would bring with them their own horses, which in turn would be used on local stock, shaping and moulding it into a formidable warhorse.

When the Moors invaded Spain in 710-711AD, they took possession of most of the sun-drenched Iberian Peninsula and named it Al-Andalus.

The Moors were renowned cavalrymen and their horses were notoriously fearless. They invaded the region from Algeria and Morocco, crossing the Strait of Gibralter into Spain and bringing with them

their native Berber, or Barb, horses. However, the journey would have been arduous and it is not known how many of the horses were successfully transported, or whether the invaders obtained their mounts from existing Iberian stock.

Indeed, Lady Sylvia Loch, author of The Royal Horse of Europe, states: "It is now almost conclusively established that the Barb horse developed as a breed from primitive Sorraia stock which gradually migrated from Spain and Portugal into North Africa in prehistoric times. Contrary to popular opinion, therefore, the Iberian horse was the likely forefather to the Barb and not vice versa.

"It would be more accurate to say that at the time of the Moorish conquest, Barb blood was reintroduced to the Iberian Peninsula."

Iberian

The Andalusian takes his name from this region but, like his close cousin, the Lusitano, he is often referred to as Pura Raza Espanola — Pure-bred Spanish Horse, or PRE. They were only recognized as two distinct breeds about 60 years ago.

Handsome and fearless, the Andalusian was the cavalry's choice — his powerful quarters enabled him to turn on the proverbial dime; his natural athleticism and turn of speed combined with biddablity made him a mount without equal.

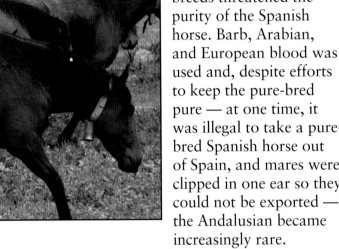

Although he fell out of favor for a short while when the heavily armored knights of the time needed a stronger, stockier mount, with the introduction of firearms the Spanish horses were again greatly in demand.

In 1667, the Duke of Newcastle wrote of the Andalusian: "He is the noblest horse in the world, the most beautiful that can be. He is of great spirit and of great courage and docile; hath the proudest trot and the best action in his trot, the loftiest gallop, and is the lovingest and gentlest horse, and fittest of all for a king in his day of triumph."

The horse of kings indeed, yet this glorious creature was almost lost, as out-crossing to other breeds threatened the purity of the Spanish horse. Barb, Arabian, and European blood was used and, despite efforts to keep the pure-bred pure — at one time, it was illegal to take a pure-bred Spanish horse out of Spain, and mares were clipped in one ear so they could not be exported — the Andalusian became increasingly rare.

An order of Carthusian monks is credited with saving the Andalusian. At the Monastry of Carthuja on the coast near Jerez de la Frontera, founded in 1476, the monks kept a small herd of pure-bred horses from which they bred carefully and selectively, preserving the

Iberian

best and the purest.

Today's horse retains his ancient nobility and aristocracy. Some 80 percent of Andalusians are gray, with 15 percent bay, and about five percent black. Although there are Oriental aspects to his fine head, in his large liquid eye and comma-shaped nostrils, his profile is convex rather than concave. He has a luxuriant, often wavy, mane and tail — mares' manes are clipped or pulled, but the stallions keep their crowning glory — and his legs are well-boned and strong to carry his powerful frame.

His days as a warhorse are over, but he excels in the bullrings of Spain and his influence can be seen in the Lipizzaners in the world-renowned Spanish Riding School of Vienna, where the famed "airs above the ground" echo the offense and defense manoeuvers of battle.

Like the Andalusian, the Lusitano is a horse of great beauty, although he lacks some of the presence of his Spanish cousin. Aficionados claim the Lusitano is more "pure" than the Andalusian, in whom the Arabian influence is more perhaps apparent, but there are few differences between the two breeds.

The breed is named for the old word for Portugal, Lusitania, but the term was not officially recognized until 1966. He has the Andalusian's power and temperament, as well as his willingness and intelligence. At an average 16hh, the Lusitano stands a little taller and is more "on the leg" — meaning there is more air between his body and the ground — and his Roman (convex) profile is more pronounced.

Once a warhorse like his cousin, he too found his place in the bullring, although the Portuguese variety differs from the Spanish in that the fight is

Iberian

conducted entirely on horseback, and it is considered a great disgrace to the rejoneadores (bullfighters) if their horses are injured.

Gray is again the predominant color, with bay, black, and chestnut also seen, as well as the occasional dun, and a distinctive mulberry shade.

These unusual colorings are thought to be a throwback to the Sorraia, from whom it is believed the Spanish horses originally developed.

Rather plain and coarse, the Sorraia in turn resembles the now extinct Tarpan and Pzrewalski's Horse, but — although he only stands between 12-14hh — his conformation makes him a horse, not a pony.

He lacks the noble good looks of the Andalusian and Lusitano, his head rather long and plain and his croup more sloping than is desirable, but he is a hardy and agile creature, able to survive on meagre rations. His name comes from the Rivers Sor and Raia, which run through Portugal and Spain — he is also sometimes called Marismeno, which translates as

"little horse of the swamp".

He is always dun or "grullo" — a distinctive grayish dun shade — and these unusual colorways sometimes appear in the wild Mustangs of America, who owe their existence to the little Iberian horse.

The fourth Iberian breed, the Alter-Real, is an interloper compared with his more ancient cousins, having been developed in the 18th century as a riding and carriage horse for the Royal Stables at Lisbon — the "Real" part of his name means "royal".

Established in 1748 in the province of Alentajo, the stud was moved to Alter — hence the first part of the breed's name — where the mineral-rich soil and good grazing was to prove beneficial. The breed was founded on 300 Andalusian mares, imported from Jerez in southern Spain, and Arabian stallions. The resulting horses were always bay — thus perfectly matched for pulling the royal carriages — standing about 15-16 hands, with a small, neat head, strong shoulders, and short, deep body.

EUROPEAN

European

Arabian and Iberian influences are clearly evident in Europe's horse and pony breeds, from the dished face of the Welsh Mountain pony to the noble splendor of the Lipizzaner, thought to be Europe's oldest equine breed.

The horse's fortunes have waxed and waned with those of this volatile continent and he has played a major role in her shifting boundaries. Wars have been fought on his back and kingdoms won and lost.

Indeed, the two World Wars of the 20th century were almost the author of the Lipizzaner's demise. Renowned for his combination of elegance and fire in the baroque glory of the Spanish Riding School of Vienna, the Lipizzaner — Austria's dancing white horse — was a triumph of selective breeding.

In the 1500s, Austria was a major European power, with an empire stretching from Switzerland to Hungary, Bohemia and Croatia, and her horses were vital — for the Cavalry, agriculture, transport, and for the Court of Hapsburg.

The best Andalusian, Barb and Berber horses were used to establish a stud in Lipizza (now Lipica) — a village 1,300 feet above sea level and to the north-west of Trieste, a harbor town in what was later known as Yugoslavia — on the edict of Archduke Charles II in 1580. These horses were bred to the local Karst stock, which were small, white, slow to mature, but very tough. It is believed the Lipizzaner inherited his flamboyant, high-stepping gait from the Karst stock, rather than his Spanish antecedents.

The Lipizza horses were moved three times during the Napoleonic Wars between Austria and France — Napolean himself gained possession of them, and bred them to his own Arabian stallion, Vesir. Other Arabian

European

blood was later introduced, as was Kladruby — two of the Lipizzaner lines, Maestro and Favory, were developed from the latter. These two were later joined by another four stallion lines — Siglavy, Neapolitano, Pluto, and Conversano — and a further two from Croatia and Hungary, Tulipan and Incitato.

Up until the early 1900s, the stud remained a private possession of the Hapsburgs and, whenever warfare had threatened the stud, the horses were moved away. During the Great War of 1914-18, the breeding stock was moved to Laxenburg, near Vienna, while foals were placed in another imperial stud, Kladrub. When Europe was reorganized after the war, the huge Austro-Hungarian Empire was split into three and the remaining 208 horses of Lipizzaner were similarly redistributed.

The Hapsburg monarchy collapsed in November 1918 and the region was divided into several smaller states, all of which vied for the ownership of the Lipizzaner herd, which was divided between Austria and Italy. A new stud was eventually established at Piper, just outside Graz in southern Austria.

With the outbreak of World War II, the Piber Stud was requisitioned by the German Army, which used it for breeding military horses. In 1941, Piber's pure-bred mares were sent to Hostau in Bohemia — which was to become part of Czechoslovakia — by the German High Command. They were rescued by a unit of General Patton's American Army in May 1945 and returned to Piber, where the stud remains to this day.

There are now only about 3,000 pure Lipizzaner horses in the world, and their glorious combination of courage, strength, athleticism,

European

temperament, and intelligence is best illustrated by the "High School" classical movements of the dancing white stallions in the Spanish Riding School of Vienna.

Spanish blood is also evident in the Friesian horse of The Netherlands, who has inherited the high knee action and proud bearing of his Andalusian forebears. He is handsome rather than beautiful, but has the long, flowing mane of the Iberian horse and the small, fine head of the Arabian, who was also used on early Friesians. However, for the past two centuries, the Friesian has been bred pure, making a remarkably uniform breed.

He is always black, with no white markings, and makes a splendid coach horse — there is little more spectacular sight than four perfectly matched black horses proudly pulling a fine carriage.

Friesians were exported to the New Amsterdam region in what was to be the United States of America in 1625 — advertisements at the time offered horses of "Dutch descent", which were almost certainly Friesians. Indeed, it has been suggested that the first Morgan horse was a Friesian, and there is some resemblence between the two breeds.

In turn, it is thought that the Friesian also influenced English breeds, including the powerful Shire horse and the Dales and Fell ponies.

The precursor to the Shire horse, the world's tallest draught horse breed, is the Old English Black, who in turn descended from the medieval Great Horse, brought to England by William the Conqueror in 1066. The English Black was the product of crossing the older breed with imported horses from the Netherlands during the 17th century.

European

By the late 1800s, however, when the breed society was founded, "black" was a misnomer and the name was changed to English Cart Horse; Shire was adopted later in 1886. Handsome, strong, and sound, the Shire horse was highly prized — during the Great Depression, pure-bred foals were known as "rent-payers".

The Shire's northern cousin, the Clydesdale, looks similar, although it is a separate breed. He takes his name from the River Clyde in Lanarkshire, Scotland, a region that used to be known as Clydesdale. He is a compact but powerful creature, slightly smaller than the Shire but having the same noble head and long, arching neck. He also has the characteristic feather — long, silky hair below the knees and hocks —and is renowned for having superb feet.

The adage "no foot, no horse" could equally well apply to the Cleveland Bay, from Yorkshire, England — Britain's oldest horse breed. He was based on the ancient packhorses, locally known as "Chapman" horses, the name Chapman being given to the packmen and travelling pedlars of the time.

Later infusions of Barb blood created a strong, versatile horse in great demand to pull carts and carriages. As his name suggests, he is always bay, with black points, making it easy to find a matched pair or four. The addition of Thoroughbred blood gave him elegance and bearing, and he became known as the Yorkshire Coach Horse, who was highly popular with the rich and the royal. England's Queen Elizabeth II uses Cleveland Bays for ceremonial duties.

Today, there are few Cleveland Bays, and he is listed by the Rare Breeds Survival Trust as "critical". However, for uniform good looks, power and versatility — as a driving horse, police

European

horse, competition horse or hunter — he is hard to beat.

Arguably the best hunters, however, are the product of an Irish Draught crossed with Thoroughbred. An ancient breed, the Irish Draught's origins lay as much in agriculture as in battle. Ireland's original stock was influenced by Anglo-Norman warhorses and later by Spanish blood — a result of trade between southern Ireland and the Iberian peninsular. But it was the farming practices in the mid 1800s that did more to shape the modern Irish Draught. Agriculture was mixed, and the Irish farmer needed a versatile horse who could work the land, pull the cart to church on Sundays, and take the farmer hunting — going all day and jumping everything in his path.

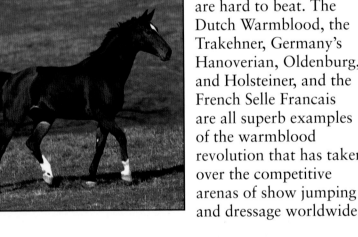

A century of selective breeding has resulted in a sound, strong, sensible horse, with considerable stamina and the ability to find a "fifth" leg when

jumping. When crossed with the Thoroughbred, he produces what used to be known as the Irish hunter, but now — as equestrianism leans ever more towards the competition arena — the cross is called the Irish Sport Horse.

For a superlative competition horse, however, the equines of continental Europe are hard to beat. The Dutch Warmblood, the Trakehner, Germany's Hanoverian, Oldenburg, and Holsteiner, and the French Selle Francais are all superb examples of the warmblood revolution that has taken over the competitive arenas of show jumping and dressage worldwide.

The term warmblood is used to describe the cross between a "coldblooded" horse, a heavy draught type, and a hotblood, such as Arabian or Thoroughbred. Perhaps the best-known example is the Dutch Warmblood, a mix of German, French, and English blood with the native

stock of the Netherlands. The result is an intelligent, sound, good-looking creature who can hold his own in international competition at the highest level.

The Trakehner, one of the oldest warmblood breeds, was established in what was East Prussia in the early 1700s. Prussia's king, Wilhelm I, demanded that his Army should have faster, stronger, sounder horses than any other military force, and established a royal stud at Trakehnen in 1732. He got his wish — the Trakehner is a good-sized horse, standing up to 17 hands high, combining bone and substance with both elegance and power. His light, springy trot makes him a force to be reckoned with in the dressage arena.

East Prussia and the Trakehnen Stud ceased to exist after World War II, and the horses were used in the mass exodus from the region in 1945 when the invading Soviet Army forced their owners to flee to the West. The only means of escape was to cross a frozen bay of the Baltic Sea — many, horses and people, did not make it.

The Trakehner horse, identified by the Prussian stud's brand, was re-established in West Germany. He has also been used to add refinement to Germany's warmbloods, of which the most successful is probably the Hanoverian. The breed originated in the state of Lower Saxony, the former kingdom of Hannover in north Germany, where a stud was founded in 1735 to produce horses for the Cavalry, for agriculture, and, later, for riding.

The Hanoverian, like all warmbloods, is a substantial, attractive horse, and is typified by his light, elastic movement — a ground-covering walk, floating trot, and a smooth, rhythmic canter. He has the characteristic intelligence and calm disposition, which make him highly trainable. In the 1992 Olympics,

European

13 equestrian medals were won on Hanoverian horses.

His neighbor, the Oldenburg, was originally bred as a coach horse, started in the 16th century by Herzog Anton Günther von Oldenburg using Friesians, as well as Spanish and Italian stallions. Later, Thoroughbred blood was used to refine and develop the breed as a sport horse, further enhanced by Anglo-Norman, Trakehner, Anglo Arab, Hanoverian, Holsteiner, and Dutch sires. And enhance the breed they certainly did — the modern Oldenburg is a superb sport horse, famously represented by show jumpers Weihaiwej and Lady Weingard, and dressage horses Donnerhall and Bonfire.

Beating the Trakehner to the "oldest warmblood" title, the Holsteiner was bred in the northernmost province of Germany, Schleswig-Holstein, from the 13th century. The Count of Holstein granted grazing rights to the Uetersen monastry, and the monks bred fine horses for agriculture and the military there until the Reformation, when property of the monastries was transferred to private landowners. But the monks' work in breeding these valuable equines was continued by the land's new owners.

Thoroughbred blood, as well as that of Cleveland Bays and Yorkshire Coach Horses, was again used to refine the Holsteiner. The breed is now prevalent in show jumping, dressage, competitive driving, and eventing, and has in turn been used in the development of other warmblood breeds.

But the warmblood success story is not simply confined to Germany; France has her own exceptional equine athlete in the Selle Francais. Like his continental cousins, the Selle Francais is a mix of breeds, but is unique in that there is trotter blood in his lineage. Breeders imported Norfolk Trotters as

European

well as Thoroughbred to Normandy to use on their native stock, which resulted in two distinctive types — the French Trotter, a swift harness horse, and the Anglo-Norman saddle horse, the latter being the foundation for the Selle Francais. His name translates as French Saddle Horse, and is synonymous with speed, stamina, and agility.

While the warmbloods dominate the world's stage, it is easy to forget that Europe has some of the oldest and most striking horse breeds on the planet. The Norwegian Fjord, the Danish Knabstrup, and the Austrian Haflinger are just a few examples of the horse's glorious history.

In fact the Fjord strongly resembles 20,000-year-old cave drawings of primitive horses, and has many similar characteristics of the Przewalski, including the upright mane and dorsal stripe and zebra barring, as well as the ancient dun coloring. A unique feature, however, is that his mane is black in the inside, while white on the outside, so when trimmed, it continues the line of the dorsal stripe.

He was the primary war mount of the Vikings, and there is archeological evidence that he has been selectively bred for at least 2,000 years. It is also likely that he was influential in other breeds, include the Icelandic Horse and some of the "mountain and moorland" breeds of the United Kingdom.

For example, the Highland pony of Scotland exhibits the same primitive dun coloring with zebra barring, although he does not have the two-tone upright mane. But he is the only native pony of Great Britain who frequently exhibits these ancient markings.

Horses have been native to Scotland's mountains from at least the eighth century BD, although whether

European

they made their own way there after the retreat of the last glaciers, or were brought with prehistoric settlers is not known. They were used by the crofters — who worked small farms or "crofts" — and later as pack animals. Surefooted, stocky and strong despite their diminutive size, they are still used in the Scottish Highlands by stalkers to transport deer down from the hills. But the Highland is a versatile equine, and his quiet, docile nature makes him a perfect family all-rounder.

Scotland's other native breed, the Shetland, stands about half the height of the Highland, but belies his tiny stature with considerable strength — a Shetland pony can carry an adult with ease.

The Shetland Islands are to the north-east of Scotland, and their main industry is fishing. An early island law warns that a thief who "cuts any other man's horse-tail or mane" will be fined a sum of ten pounds — a huge amount of money when the law was passed that underlines the severity of the crime. The hair from the Shetland pony provided the raw material for fishing nets and lines.

The pony breed is thought to be at least 2,000 years old, and the harsh island conditions ensured the Shetland is tough and hardy, and able to survive in a harsh environment on meagre rations. The modern Shetland is a sturdy, stocky animal, and miniature ponies — standing only 28 inches high at the shoulder — are increasingly popular.

The American Shetland Pony Club was formed in 1888, and registers both "classic" and "modern" — the latter almost unrecognizable from the ancient survivors in Scotland's northerly islands.

Wales, too, has her own equine breeds, separated in the studbook as Ponies and Cobs. The smallest, the Welsh Mountain pony, shows clearly

the Arabian influence in his small, neat head, and concave profile. But never let it be said that he is merely a "pretty toy"; he makes an excellent riding and driving pony, and, although spirited, has a gentle nature that makes him an ideal child's mount.

The Welsh Mountain was the foundation of all the Welsh breeds — it is said that the biggest, the Cob, should in silhouette look like a scaled up version of the Mountain pony. Welsh blood has also been used as an out-cross for other native breeds, including the Dales pony. There is no upper height limit for Welsh Cobs, and Welsh part-breds also make superb competition horses and ponies.

Although he may stand only 13.2 hands high, the Haflinger of the Southern Tyrolean Mountains in Austria and northern Italy is a small horse, rather than a pony. His origins can be traced back to medieval times, when a horse of Oriental type was recorded in the region.

However, the foundation stallion of the breed, 249 Folie, wasn't foaled until 1874. His sire was a part-bred Arabian called 133 El'Bedavi XXII and his dam was a native Tyrolean mare — all pure-bred Haflingers trace back directly to Folie through seven different stallion lines — A, B, M, N, S, ST, and WT.

The modern breed is always chestnut, varying from a rich golden shade to deep chocolate, and has a white or flaxen mane and tail. He has a pretty, lean head, with large expressive eyes — evidence of his Oriental ancestry — is an all-round good-looking little horse.

Even more striking is Denmark's Knabstrupper, the so-called "Tiger Horse" of Holbaek, Nordsealand. The breed is founded, unusually, on a mare line. In 1812, Villars Lunn, who lived in a manor house called Knabstrupgaard, bought a mare named Flaebe. She had a rare beauty — a quality, dark red horse with white mane and tail, white snowflake markings on her body, and brown spots across her quarters. Her foals all inherited her extraordinary coloring, and her son, Flaebestallion, became the foundation sire.

AMERICAN

American

Given that her native horses are thought to have died out about 10,000 years ago, and equines were only reintroduced by the Spanish explorers as recently as the 16th century, the enormous diversity of equine breeds in the United States is testament to that great nation's ability to adapt and evolve.

The original horses would have travelled across the Bering land bridge that once joined Siberia to Alaska. It is not known why they died out; they were perhaps hunted to extinction, or it may well have been the last Ice Age, from which they were too slow to retreat.

But when the Spanish Conquistadors landed in the New World in the 1500s, they brought with them their own native stock. Some of these horses either escaped, were set free, or, some believe, swam ashore when the vessels carrying them were shipwrecked. Whichever, or all, is the real story, these horses formed the basis for all modern American breeds.

In the wild Mustang can be seen the occasional gray-dun or grullo coloring, a throwback to the Sorraia of Spain and Portugal; the Peruvian Paso and Paso Fino have the fire and presence of the Andalusian and Lusitano.

Perhaps the most iconic American breed is the Appaloosa, with his striking spotted coat. Vast herds of wild horses roamed the Western deserts and plains of North America, and were captured and tamed by cowboys and Native Americans alike. But it the was latter people who began to breed their horses selectively.

The Nez Perce Indians of the north-west are credited with breeding the spotted horse, using only the fastest, soundest and most surefooted — traits for which he is as famous as for his colorful appearance. But they did not give him his name. As the horse's popularity grew, people began to refer

American

to him as a "Palousey horse", taken from the Palouse River along which the native American tribes lived.

When the proud Nez Perce were finally forced to surrender to the American Army, their prized spotted horses were seized and, being diluted by other equine blood, were almost lost. It was thanks to a wheat farmer called Claude Thompson that the Appaloosa was saved — the farmer recognized the value of his striking coat and formed the Appaloosa Horse Club in 1938. There are now half a million horses registered with the club, with 13 base coat colors and seven accepted coat patterns.

The USA's other colorful equine, the Paint, was also revered by the Native Americans, who believed the two-toned creatures had magical powers. But he was equally well regarded by the cowboys, for his strength and stamina and turn of foot as much as for his flashy good looks.

There are three recognized color patterns, Tobiano, Overo and Tovero.

The Tobiano may be either predominantly dark in color or white, the dark color usually covering one or both flanks and all four legs being white, at least below the hocks and knees. He generally has regular, distinct oval or round spots that extend down over his neck and chest like a shield. His head may have a blaze, strip, star, or snip and his tail is often two colors.

The Overo, like the Tobiano, may be predominantly dark or white, but his white markings are irregular, and scattered or splashy, although they do not usually cross the back of the horse between his withers and tail, and at least one but more often all four of his legs are dark. He often has a completely white face.

A white-faced horse used to be called "bald" — hence the names

American

piebald — black and white — or skewbald — any other color and white.

The Tovero is an accepted pattern that does not fit either Tobiano or Overo, and the horse often has one blue eye or both.

The Paint horse is sometimes referred to as Pinto but this is not correct. Pinto refers to the broken-coated coloring, whereas the Paint is a registered breed.

The modern Paint horse is as highly prized today as his feral cousin was to the Native Americans and cowboys of the West, and the American Paint Horse Association strives to ensure the breed continues to thrive. For while his striking coloring makes him special, his hardiness, soundness, and general good looks make him an equine prince.

Her horses are as colorful as her history, and America is one of the few nations to recognize specific horse colors as breeds. Hence the Palomino, whose glowing coat should be the hue of a newly minted 14K gold coin, offset by a mane and tail of pure white.

The origins of the color itself are largely unknown, but golden horses were found in early China, and are depicted in Sandro Botticelli's renowned work, The Adoration of the Magi, thought to have been painted in 1475. The color found favor with Spain's Queen Isabella (1451-1504) and it is also sometimes still called Isabella.

It occurs in many modern horse breeds, but is not permitted in Arabs or Thoroughbreds.

The Buckskin, also recognized as a breed in the States, is a darker shade of palomino, and again is thought to be an ancient color. But the American horse is renowned as being "as tough as wet leather", and is noted for his strength and stamina; a Buckskin horse

American

with weak legs or bad feet is extremely rare.

There are five distinct recognized colorways: the true buckskin is the color of tanned deer hide, although it can vary from yellow to dark gold, and has black points — the ears, lower legs, and muzzle. The dun is duller than the buckskin but is nonetheless an intense color, usually with dark points and occasionally a dorsal stripe — along the spine — and bars on the legs.

The grulla also has the dorsal stripe and leg barring, and the body color can vary from mouse, blue, dove, and slate.

There is also red dun, which can range from peach to copper to a deep, rich red. Points must be chestnut or darker red, and a deep red dorsal stripe must be evident.

The final acceptable color is brindle dun, a unique coloration with stripes over the barrel of the body, with the dorsal stripe and leg bars, but occasionally teardrop-shaped body markings and zebra striping.

Perhaps almost as striking as the Buckskin is the Rocky Mountain Horse. Little is known about the origins of the breed — legend has it that, in the late 1800s, a young horse appeared at the foothills of the Appalachian Mountains in eastern Kentucky.

He was of a deep chocolate color with flaxen mane and tail, and possessed a natural, ambling four-beat gait — in addition to walk, trot, canter, and gallop — that proved ideal for working the farms of the area. He was also sweet-tempered and a good "doer", and proved a versatile all-rounder. The locals referred to him as the Rocky Mountain Horse, and the name stuck.

Gaited horses — that is, equines that possess a natural fifth gait — are

American

popular in America. It is believed that the fifth gait, variously, the single-foot, rack, pace, running walk, and fox trot, occurs naturally, and cannot be taught. These gaits are supremely comfortable for the rider, and energy conserving for the horse, who can keep them up at considerable speeds and for great distances.

The Tennessee Walking Horse, for example, is famous for his running walk, an extra-smooth gliding gait of up to 20 miles per hour. The Missouri Fox Trotter is renowned for the fox trot — a diagonal gait like the trot, but the horse appears to walk with its front legs and trot with his hind legs. Because the back feet slide, the rider experiences little jarring action and is quite comfortable to sit for long periods.

But one of the greatest success stories of American equine breeds is that of Racking, or Single-Foot, Horse. Noted for his beauty, elegance, and intelligence, this noble creature grew with the southern plantations before the Civil War. His single-footed gait proved comfortable enough to allow the plantation masters to ride across their vast acreages literally for hours.

The single-foot, or "rack", is so called because only one hoof strikes the ground at any one time, and the horse appears to jump from one foot to another. The Racking Horse undoubtedly has his origins with the Tennessee Walker, but his versatility, combined with the smooth gait, good looks, and docile nature will be preserved for future generations to enjoy — the Racking Horse Breeders' Association of America was founded in 1971.

The delightfully named Florida Cracker — another gaited breed — is also comparatively new, with the breed registry being chartered in 1989. But, like all American equines, the Cracker's origins trace back to the Spanish

American

invaders and, over time, he has been known by a variety of colorful names — Chicksaw Pony, Seminole, March Tackle, Prairie Pony, Florida Cow Pony, Grass Gut, and others.

He was an essential part of the cattle industry in Florida, which began some 500 years ago, and continues to flourish. The cowboys of the region were known as "crackers", because of the sound of their whips cracking in the air, and the name extended to their fast, agile little horses.

The Florida Cracker has the flatfoot walk, running walk, and amble, and although they are good-natured and willing, they never lack spirit.

What almost caused the Cracker's demise was the change that affected the whole of the American West, when the parasite screwworm infected the cattle herds of the Dust Bowl that moved into the east. This changed herding practice, as cowboys who had previously used their horses to herd and drive the cattle, now had to rope them to be tested and treated. Hence the lighter type of horse — the Florida Cracker — fell out of favor to the stronger, hardier Quarter Horse.

Compact, good-looking and swift, the Quarter Horse does not, as is widely believed, take his name from the quantity of Thoroughbred blood in his heritage. Often considered the first American "native", the Quarter Horse is named for his precocious speed over a quarter of a mile.

The foundation stock of the Quarter Horse were Arab, Turk and Barb horses, solid and muscular, later mixed with English Thoroughbred, which gave the explosive speed. One-on-one races were popular through the early American streets, roads, and lanes, with huge sums of money wagered on the outcome — it is rumored that entire plantations

American

changed hands on the results of these contests.

But combined with his speed was a calm disposition and a renowned "cow sense", so the Quarter Horse's popularity spread across the West and his versality ensures he remains one of the USA's most treasured equines.

The first American "native" breed the Quarter Horse may be, but the word "national" is not part of his title, as it is for the USA's own show breed. And the National Show Horse more than lives up to his name. His origins lie with the Saddlebred, called "the peacock of the show ring", and with the Arabian, from whom he inherits his elegance and grace.

The American Saddlebred descended from the Spanish stock crossed with Irish Galloways and English Hobby horses later imported to the States. These imports were naturally gaited — trotters were to become popular later — and the resulting strong and hardy little horses came to be known as Narragansett Pacers. In turn, they were crossed with Thoroughbreds, and the result was an attractive, amenable horse with poise and beauty, that was naturally gaited. By the 1700s, he was known simply as the American Horse.

Of good size and even temperament, as well as beauty and grace, he was prized as a riding and carriage horse, prized for his eagerness, kind disposition, strength, and stamina.

When horse shows first appeared in the 1800s in Kentucky and Virginia, the American Saddlebred — then known as the Kentucky Saddler — would frequently be in the ribbons.

Outcrossings to Arabian, Morgan, and further Thoroughbred blood had enhanced his good looks, but he retained his sweet nature and his gaits, which include the rack (single-foot).

American

It was later outcrossings to Arabian blood that produced the American National Show Horse, a charismatic creature with the Arabian flash and fire and the Saddlebred's inherent kindness. The National Show Horse Registry was formed in 1982, and Arabian blood in registered horses can range from 25 percent to 99 percent.

Although the Saddlebred has a lot to thank the Arabian for, it is thought that about 90 percent of modern Saddlebreds also carry Morgan blood.

The history of the Morgan horse is one of the best American success stories, and by many he is considered to be the first truly "American" breed.

His story begins in West Spring, Massachusetts, in 1789 with a bay colt called Figure, who was given to a schoolmaster called Justin Morgan as part payment of a debt. He was a comparatively small horse — which is thought to be why his new owner kept him, rather than sell him on; bigger horses were more in vogue at the time — but was immensely strong and fast, as well as easy-keeping.

His exact breeding is unknown, but he is thought to have been by a stallion called True Briton, and may be been a Thoroughbred-Welsh Cob cross.

As tales of his prowess spread, he became known, as was the custom of the day, as the Justin Morgan horse. He died in 1821 at the age of 32, have left a legacy of "Morgan horses".

The modern Morgan is a compact, good-looking horse who combines elegance and grace with strength and stamina. He was a popular cavalry mount, and today finds favor in the showring and hunting field, as well as competing successfully in dressage, show jumping, endurance, and eventing.

Another breed to be founded on one horse was the Pony of the Americas, who owes his existance to a striking colt called Black Hand. Born in 1954, he was the result of an Arab-Appaloosa mare bred to a Shetland stallion. His owner, a Mason City, Iowa, pony breeder and lawyer called Les Boomhower named him Black Hand for the spots on his white flank that formed a definite handprint.

WORLD

World

It is a testament to the horse's ability to adapt and evolve that he is found - in some form - in almost all four corners of the globe. From the sturdy little Icelandic, who has played a major role in the history of Europe's least populated country; to the lithe Kathiawari of India; the Nooitgedachter of Africa, and the Java Pony of Indonesia, the world's horse breeds are as diverse and varied as her climate and terrain.

The Icelandic, although he stands little more than 13 hands high, is always called a horse — there is no Icelandic word for pony. His history dates back to the ninth century, with the settlement of the Vikings, who brought with them their horses of mostly Germanic descent, although there are suggestions that there an indigenous breed of horse, called Equus Scandinavia.

To the Norse people, the horse was held in the highest regard; he featured in their myths and stories, their gods owned fleet-footed equines on which to defeat their enemies, and, today, many horse herds in Iceland are named for these mythical creatures.

To the Viking, the horse was equally vital, an indispensable partner in war and thus granted great respect. Slain warriors were often buried beside their mounts.

For centuries, the horse was the only form of transport on Iceland, and even with the introduction of the automobile, in 1904, the islanders continued to breed their tough little horses. Forty different colors are seen in the Icelandic, with 100 variations, but the breed has been kept pure and disease-free for centuries — no importation of horses nor any other livestock is permitted, and all used tack and riding wear is only allowed if it is fully disinfected.

World

There are now about 80,000 horses in Iceland, which — with the human population of around 270,000 — works out at more than three people per Icelandic horse.

The Falabella of Argentina is even smaller than the Icelandic, but he, too, is a horse, not a pony. Like all the horse breeds of the Americas his origins are Spanish; vast herds of semi-feral horses were left to wander the great plains and to survive as best they could. The Pampas of Argentina was harsh and unforgiving, and only the toughest and most resilient flourished in the area, undergoing genetic mutations and changes dictated by the climate and conditions.

In the mid-19th century, the Falabella family of Buenos Aries noticed in the horse herds of the Mupache Indians a noticeably smaller but well-balanced equine — a horse perfectly formed in miniature. Years of selective breeding by the family — introducing blood from, among others, Shetland and Welsh Ponies — has produced today's Falabella, a beautifully proportioned miniature horse who stands between 28 inches to about 32 inches at the shoulder.

Another breed to take the name of its originator is the Campolina of Brazil, developed by Cassiano Campolina in the 1870s on his Fazenda Tamque farm. He was given a black mare named Medeia who, put to an Andalusian stallion, foaled a dark gray colt called Monarca, who was to be the foundation sire of the Campolina horse, serving as a stallion on the farm for 25 years. The breed was continued after the death of Senor Campolina, with blood from Anglo-Norman, Clydesdale, American Saddle Horse, Holsteiner, and Mangalarga Marchador, the so-called National Horse of Brazil.

World

Perhaps South America's most well-known breed is the Peruvian Paso, sometimes confused with the Paso Fino, but an entirely separate breed.

He is a mixture of all the best characteristics of his ancestors — the easy temperament of the Jennet, the spirit and strength of the Barb, and the beauty and nobility of the Andalusian. The overall impression is of muscular power, combined with proud elegance. He carries his head high, and has the flashy knee action to catch the eye in the show ring. A gaited breed, he passes on this ability to his offspring, and also exhibits the unique "termino" — a front-leg movement that suggests the loose outward roll of a swimmer's arms in front crawl.

But most important of all, he has "brio" — that indefinable "look at me" quality as he performs with exuberance and more than a small dash of arrogance.

The Paso Fino does bear a striking resemblance to his Peruvian cousin, and exhibits the same extravagant movement - his name means "horse of the fine step". He has the fine head and proud carriage of his Spanish ancestors, and his spirit is tempered with a gentle and sensible nature.

Coveted by kings, hidden for centuries, a survivor of the Ark? Well, perhaps. The little Persian horse, or Caspian, is known to be an ancient breed, some even suggesting that he was used to develop the Arabian, rather than the other way round.

In well-documented searches for Noah's Ark, some historians believe the Ark's final resting place was high in the mountain ranges of northern Iran — which used to be called Persia. And at the base of these mountains, the first remains of the Caspian horse were found. Is it possible that the little equine walked, two by two, off the Ark itself 5,000 years ago?

World

A romantic fantasy maybe, but it is known that these small, neat horses existed in Iran in the Mesolithic Period, refuting the former, widely held, belief that horses were introduced to the region in the third or early second millennium BC.

He is depicted in ancient Persian art dating back to 3,000 BC — appearing on such celebrated artifacts as the stone frieze in the Palace of Persepolis; the seal of King Darius The Great in 550 BC, and the Gold Oxus Treasure of Darabgird, on which four small horses pull a ceremonial chariot.

The horses on all these artworks are remarkably similar — Arabian in appearance, but of diminutive size, with small, concave heads, neat ears, and slim legs. In short, the Caspian horse.

And yet this beautiful, versatile breed was almost lost. After the Great War of 637 AD, the court of Persia was destroyed, and her tiny wild horses were lost. It wasn't until 1965, when Louise Firouz, an American living in Iran, found a herd of about 30 small horses living near the Caspian Sea. She recognized them as being extraordinarily similar to the horses on the Palace of Persepolis frieze. It is due to her dedication and determination to save this tiny piece of living history that saved the regal Persian breed from extinction.

One of the rarest breeds in the world, however, is South Africa's exotically named Nooitgedachter, a magnificent descendent of the Basuto Pony, which in turn was developed from the Cape Horse of Lesotho, a survivor of the freezing winters and blazing summers.

The harsh climate produced a remarkably resilient little equine, agile, courageous, and hardy. He had strong joints and hard feet, and an innate surefootedness, which gave him unique

World

ability to traverse the country's rough terrain. And he had a natural affection for, and affinity to, man, as well as intelligence and stamina.

These characteristics made the Cape Horse and, later, the Basuto, an exceptional Cavalry mount. Indeed, during the Boer War (1899-1902) these horses served Boer and Briton with equal fortitude.

But despite — or perhaps because of — his worldwide fame for endurance and valor, the Basuto was almost extinct in Lesotho by the 1940s.

The South African Department of Agriculture bought a small herd of horses in 1951 and established an intensive and highly selective breeding program at the Nooitgedachter Research Station near Ermelo. In 1976, the Nooitgedachter was recognized as South Africa's first indigenous equine breed.

Handsome, hardy, and extremely versatile, the Nooitgedachter excels in almost every equestrian discipline.

His close cousin the Boer Pony, or Horse, said to be as old as white civilization itself.

The first Dutch settlers of Cape Town — the "Mother City" of South Africa — imported equines from Java, Indonesia, and to avoid too close inbreeding, brought in Arabian horses and, from Argentina, the nearest port, Andalusians. Later, some English Thoroughbred blood was added.

The Boer War, the Great Trek of 1836, when Boer families and their servants struck out to colonize the High Veld, and an equine illness — probably African Horse Sickness, which is still a fatal disease — all contributed to the Boer Horse's downfall, wiping them out in their thousands. But the breed remains,

World

in greatly diminished numbers.

The Java Pony of Indonesia, used in the development of the Boer breed, is believed to be Chinese in origin, later influenced by Arabian and Barb blood, introduced to the island in the 17th century. But there is little to suggest this in his rather coarse appearance, although he appears to have the Barb's toughness, and he is rarely adversely affected by the extreme heat. He is tough and willing, thrives on meagre rations, apparently tireless, and his strength belies his height. He is still used on Java to pull the "sados", the island's two-wheeled taxis, which are often buried under their cargo of people and luggage.

In order to improve the somewhat unprepossessing looks of the Java Pony, Batak blood was introduced, albeit with limited success. The Batak horses were held in high esteem, each clan owning three, which were sacred and dedicated to a trinity of gods.

The horses were allowed to graze and wander at will and, at the end of their lives, were sacrificed to the gods, with a younger animal taking their place.

The Batak is noticeably more Arabian in character than his Javanese cousin, and today is used as a working animal, as well as providing important upgrades for Indonesian horse breeding.

Arabian influences are also clear in the beautiful Kathiawari Horse of the Indian subcontinent. It is known that a native stock existed in India well before the time of the Moghul Emperors (1526-1857). These horses, of mixed quality, were found in the provinces down the west coast as far as Maharashtra, descended from breeds like the Kabuli and Baluchi, northern equines related to the steppe and desert horses in the west and north-west of Asia. These horses, of the "dry" desert type, were spare and lean, with curved ears.

World

These curling ears are pronounced in the Kathiawari, and his close cousin, the Marwari, although the latter is a distinctly separate breed. He looks like an Arabian, but for his charming curled ears that touch at the tips, and which are remarkably mobile, able to turn through 360°.

The Kathiawari is the horse of princes — bred in royal households of the Kathiawar Peninsula on the western coast. He was a cherished royal pet, prized for his extravagant beauty and his intelligence, docility, and affectionate nature. The royal households bred the "Kattywar" horse selectively, specializing in their own particular strain, which were usually named after the foundation mare. Even now, there are 28 such strains still recognized.

More prosaically, the Kathiawari, once also deployed as a Cavalry horse, is now used widely in India as a police horse.

World

WILD & FERAL

Wild & Feral

With his distinctive dun coloring, black dorsal stripe, zebra barring, and upright, bristly mane, Przewalski's Horse — or the Asiatic Wild Horse — most closely resembles the wild horses of 20,000 years ago that extensively roamed Europe and Asia. Cave drawings of that time found in France and Spain depict these horses in far larger quantities than any other mammal, so it is safe to assume they were abundant.

Man hunted them for food — also depicted in cave drawings — but as he began to tame his environment, with rudimentary agriculture and livestock practices being introduced, the wild horses became pests. They devoured cultivated crops and broke through fences, and wild stallions would "steal" mares kept for meat. As agriculture spread, and more land was fenced off, the wild herds were driven further into areas that were unsuitable for cultivation.

Later, man realized the usefulness of the horse — not just as a meal on the hoof — and the wild herds were depleted further. Today, there are few true wild horses left, most — such as the Mustang of America and the Brumby of Australia — being more correctly called feral, that is domesticated horses that have escaped back into the wild.

By the 19th century, the only wild horse herds left were in Poland and Southern Russia, although there was some debate as to whether they were truly wild, or in fact feral.

But in 1879, a wild herd was discovered in the Tachin Schah — the "Mountains of the Yellow Horses" — on the edge of the Gobi Desert by the explorer Nikolai Mikhailovitch Przewalski, a colonel in the Imperial Russian Army. The horses were known by the local people as Taki, and were hunted for their meat almost to the point of extinction.

Wild & Feral

Przewalski is widely credited for the discovery of the breed — and it was named after him — but very similar equines are described by English naturalist Colonel Hamilton Smith in 1814.

Przewalski's Horse is unique among equines in that he has 66 chromosomes rather than 64. He has the primitive color and markings of dun with cream-colored belly, black legs, points, and dorsal stripe, and upright mane — also black — with no forelock.

Spain and Portugal's Sorraia Pony is thought to be a direct ascendant from the Przewalski, and he does display the same primitive dun coloring. This distinctive coat also appears occasionally in America's Mustang, a throwback to his Spanish origins. His name comes from the Spanish mesteno, meaning "stray or ownerless horse". To the Native Americans, the horse — a creature they had never seen before — inspired fear and awe, but they soon overcame their initial reactions and gentled him, tamed him, and rode him into raids and battle.

The Mustang was so plentiful that the Indian people didn't bother to corral their horses, but let them roam free, either recapturing them or "liberating" horses from the Spanish settlements. As a result the horses bred indiscriminately and, by 1900, there were an estimated two million at large.

To the ranchers, they were considered a pest and were slaughtered in such numbers that, by 1970, there were fewer than 17,000 left. In 1971, Congress passed the Wild Free-Roaming Horse and Burro Act, and today there are thought to be about 41,000, protected as "living symbols of the historic and pioneer spirit of the West".

The ponies of Assateague — the island off the coast of Virginia and Maryland — are, like the Mustang,

Wild & Feral

of Spanish origin, and legend has it they are survivors of a shipwreck who swam ashore to safety. The romance of the breed was further enhanced by Marguerite Henry's children's classic, Misty of Chincoteague, published in 1947.

The ponies of Assateague and Chincoteague — the latter translates as "beautiful land across the water" — are essentially the same breed, the two islands being separated by a narrow channel. The ponies would swim across this from Assateague, the larger of the two islands, to Chincoteague to raid the farmers' crops.

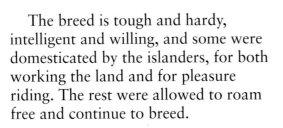

The breed is tough and hardy, intelligent and willing, and some were domesticated by the islanders, for both working the land and for pleasure riding. The rest were allowed to roam free and continue to breed.

Today, there is an annual pony penning, an immensely popular tourist attraction that began in 1924, on the last Wednesday and Thursday of July, when the ponies of Assateague are rounded up and swam across the channel. The foals and some adults are auctioned off on the Thursday, and any unsold ponies swim back to Assateague.

Equally at home in his watery environment is the Camargue pony of southern France, who lives in the marshlands of the Rhone delta. Indeed, so well has he adapted to this harsh region — which is either scorched by baking sun or whipped by icy winds — that he is often called the "horse of the sea".

He is an ancient breed, thought to be descended from the now extinct Soutré horse, whose remains have been found in the Rhone delta, but he may equally have been influenced by Army horses brought to the region by the Greeks, Romans, and Arabs. It is just

Wild & Feral

as possible that these Armies captured the indigenous horses and took them home, so the Camargue may have played a part in the development of early breeds.

The Camargue is always gray, the foals being born black or brown and lightening with age; the lighter the color, the older the horse. He is a small, sturdy creature, even tempered but lively, agile, and brave. He makes a superb riding horse, his instinctive surefootedness perfectly suited to the terrain, and his athleticism and courage makes him invaluable in herding the fierce little black bulls of southern France.

England's semi-feral moorland breeds, the Exmoor and the Dartmoor, are also prime examples of how the horse can adapt to survive. The Exmoor, who inhabits the moorland of the same name in the south-west of the country, is a primitive type who has remained largely unchanged, the remoteness of the moor meaning that very little outside blood has been introduced.

Exmoor itself was formerly a designated Royal Forest — used as a hunting ground — until 1818, when it was sold off. Several people continued to breed the true Exmoor Pony, and today the breed remains remarkably uniform.

He under 13 hands high and is always brown, although of varied shades. He has darker legs and a "mealy" muzzle, oatmeal coloring that also appears around the eyes and on his underbelly. He has the primitive "toad" eye, a unique hood that protects the eye from the wet and cold, and an "ice" tail, which has a thick fanlike growth of short hair at the top, channelling water away from his rump. His winter coat grows in two layers, providing "thermal underwear" beneath and a "raincoat" — coarse, greasy water-repellent hair — above.

This efficient double layer also allows for "snow-hatching", letting snow build up on the pony's coat because insufficient body heat escapes to melt it. The pony's body is not chilled by melting snow; he simply shakes off the build up.

Like the Exmoor, the Dartmoor is an ancient breed — the earliest known reference to a Dartmoor Pony appeared in the will of a Saxon bishop, Aeflwold of Crediton, Devon, in 1012. But he has had a much more chequered history, having been crossed with a variety of different breeds, including Shetland and Welsh Mountain ponies, Arabian, and a Polo Pony.

During World War II, when Dartmoor was used as a training area and its ponies deemed ideal for target practice, the breed hovered on the brink of extinction, but was saved by a few dedicated breeders. Today, his amenable nature and stocky good looks make him an ideal child's pony, although he is still listed as "vulnerable" by the Rare Breeds Survival Trust.

Australia's wild horse breed, the Brumby, is also under threat, although largely for his own good.

Immortalized by books and films, the antipodean feral horse — equines are not indigenous to Australia, but were brought over by settlers in the 1700s — has been allowed to breed indiscriminately and is considered a pest. Of little use as a riding or stock horse because of his intractable nature and often inferior conformation, he damages fences, competes with domestic cattle for grazing, and depletes and fouls water supplies.

The wild horses may also mate with domestic equines, spreading disease.

Subsequently, there are frequent Brumby culls, which are viewed by animal welfare groups as inhumane. However, culls are necessary, not just for the sake of the farmers and cattle ranchers, but also to protect the Brumby himself. If left to breed without check, many horses may die of thirst or starvation.

WORKING

Working

He has been our most constant companion. He has been with us in war — and has perished alongside our comrades in the blood and mud of the battleground. He has rejoiced with us in celebrations, and drawn the carriages of our monarchs. He has patrolled our city streets as a police horse to keep them — and us — safe. He has helped us plough our fields to grow sustenance for our own and for our future generations. He has been our eager partner in our leisure hours, and in our pursuit of glory on the world's stage — or in local riding club competitions.

As Ronald Duncan says in his famous poem,

The Horse:

He serves without servility;
He has fought without enmity.
There is nothing so powerful,
Nothing less violent;
There is nothing so quick,
> *Nothing more patient.*
> *England's past has*
> *been borne on his back.*

For almost as long as man has fought man — and in whichever corner of the globe — the horse has fought with him, and died with him. Statues of fallen heroes on horseback tell their own story — if the horse has one front leg raised, his rider died of injuries sustained on the battlefield; if the horse has both legs raised, his rider died where he fell. If the horse is standing foursquare, his rider passed on through natural causes.

Working

It was the skill of the Iberian horsemen who invaded the European peninsula that prompted the famous Greek cavalry officer, Xenophon, to praise the "gifted Iberian horses" and the part they played in Sparta's defeat of Athenians around 450 BC. In the second Punic War (218-201 BC), Hannibal fought off the invading Roman Army — not once but on several occasions — through the use of Iberian horses.

And these horses — courageous, spirited, and biddable — continued to feature heavily in battle. William the Conqueror rode an Iberian horse in the Battle of Hastings in 1066.

There are almost as many stories of bravery on behalf of horses as there are of men in the battlefield. In Custer's Last Stand, for example, after the Battle of Little Big Horn, all his men were annihilated, but the other half of the regiment — divided by Custer before the battle — found one horse still alive.

The horse, a gelding called Comanche, was discovered with seven arrows in his body. He was sent to Fort Lincoln, Dakota, where, with treatment and care, he made a full recovery. He was then given the freedom of the fort's grounds. Although he was never again ridden, he was saddled for all ceremonial occasions, and became a national celebrity.

In the American Civil War, some horses became as famous as their partners, whether Confederate or Union.

General Thomas Jonathan "Stonewall" Jackson acquired a former Union officer's mount, a mare called Old Sorrel. Because of her size — she was so small that the General's feet almost touched the ground — she was often known as Little Sorrel. Stonewall was riding Old Sorrel when he was mortally wounded.

General Robert Lee's horse Traveller was perhaps the most famous of the Civil War. He was a Saddlebred and

Working

is the supposed "author" of a ghost-written story of the Civil War seen through a horse's eyes.

Union soldiers also relied on their horses. Major General Joseph Hooker — "Fighting Joe" — acquired a horse called Lookout at Chattanooga who stood a massive 17 hands high and was much cherished by his master.

A horse called Moscow was equally favored by Major General Philip Kearny, but he was a white horse and therefore too easy a target, so Kearny switched to a bay.

Colonel Philip Sheridan — or "Little Phil", because he stood only five feet five inches tall — famous for his ride to Winchester to rally his men who were retreating from a surprise attack, renamed the steed who carried him there after the scene of the battle. It is immortalized in the poem Sheridan's Ride:

…With foam and with dust the black charger was gray;
By the flash of his eye, and the red nostril's play,
He seemed to the whole great Army to say, "I have brought you Sheridan all the way From Winchester, down to save the day!"

Hurrah! Hurrah for Sheridan!
Hurrah! Hurrah for horse and man!
And when their statues are placed on high,
Under the dome of the Union sky,
The American soldier's Temple of Fame;
There with the glorious general's name,
Be it said, in letters both bold and bright,
"Here is the steed that saved the day
By carrying Sheridan into the fight,
From Winchester, 20 miles away!"

Working

With increasing mechanization, and man's conquering of the skies, the horse in war became part of the world's history. And those commemorative statues are as much a tribute to him as to his fallen masters.

Even in peacetime, the horse has a working role. He is still widely used by police forces — in the April of 2006, the New York Police Department announced it was to double the number of "four-legged officers". Dubbed "10 foot cops", police horses in New York are said to be able to do the work of 10 patrolmen, and the department planned to expand the number of horses from 85 to 160 over a three-year period.

Mounted police must have at least five years' patrol experience, and to have unblemished service, disciplinary, and attendance records. They undergo 12 weeks' training.

The horses, too, have to be exceptional. They must be spirited but calm, strong but trainable, intelligent, and brave. And above all, they must obey.

Police horses were introduced in New York in 1871 and, by 1904, there were 400 horses on duty. But as motor vehicles became increasingly popular, the numbers dwindled to 40, and the unit was almost disbanded in the 1970s.

But the 10 foot cop has the advantage in crowd control, having the psychological benefits of being able to see those at the back of a crowd as well as those at the front. Mounted officers are deployed across many American states, dealing with riots, rallies, rowdy students, concerts, and political conventions. There are tens of thousands of police horses across the United States.

In Canada, of course, they are the Royal Canadian Mounted Police (RCMP), famous for "always getting

Working

their man", and proud of their motto: "Uphold the right".

It was the Cypress Hill Massacre of 1873 that led to the creation of Canada's police force. Fur traders blamed a local tribe of North American Indians — known by Canadians as the First Nation — called the Assiniboine for the disappearance of some of their horses, and proceeded to shoot them all dead, despite their innocence.

Appalled by this atrocity, the government, headed by Canada's first Prime Minister, Sir John A Macdonald, pushed through legislation to create a national police force. The first North-West Mounted Police (NWMP) comprised 300 men. By 1903, King Edward VII recognized the work of the force and bestowed them "Royal" status. The name was changed to the Royal Canadian Mounted Police in 1920, but they are more colloquially known — worldwide — as Mounties.

Canada's police were based on mounted forces of England, and police horses are as much a part of her Capital City as Buckingham Palace, St Paul's Cathedral, and the Tower of London. A spectacular sight on London's streets, the police horse is far from merely window dressing. Here, too, he is used for crowd control, and is sometimes injured in the course of duty.

In May 2002, during disturbances when fans rioted after a football match, an eight-year-old horse called Alamain severed an artery in his leg when he reared up and fell onto a car when a firecracker exploded beneath him. Fortunately, his life was saved, but another 25 police horses were also injured in the violence.

It was violence of a different kind that marked one of the most horrific incidences in the history of working horses in the United Kingdom. In 1982, seven horses were killed when a nail

Working

bomb set by the Irish Republican Army (IRA) went off as officers from the Queen's Lifeguard — a detachment of her Household Cavalry — were passing in London's Hyde Park. Two men and seven horses were killed in the atrocity, and another, Sefton, was so severely injured that he required eight hours of surgery. Sefton survived and, on his retirement, lived to the age of 30. Today, his name is synonymous with bravery under attack.

In happier times, however, the Household Cavalry mounted regiment is the epitome of pomp and circumstance, undertaking ceremonial duties on State and Royal occasions, and performing the spectacular Musical Ride that thrills cheering crowds across the land.

The Ride is performed by troopers in full dress mounted on black horses; four "rough riders" in the stable dress of the 1800s; four trumpeters mounted on gray horses, and one on a splendid piebald or skewbald drumhorse. The display is a carefully choreographed program to music, including columns of riders crossing each other at full gallop.

No less spectacular is the horse's role in the circus ring. Easy to train, quick to learn, and eager to please, he is a natural performer, from the tiny but strong Shetland Pony, to the flamboyant Andalusian, with his flowing mane and tail, to the elegant Arabian. Circuses everywhere have equine performers in the ring, and they are a joy to behold.

But never let it be said that the horse is a "one-trick pony". His great physical strength — once essential to work the land — is still exploited by man. Indeed, ploughing matches — where the skill of the ploughman is every bit as important as the speed of his horses — are enormously popular in England, Scotland, Ireland, and Canada.

Working

But you will find the working horse everywhere, be it in the tourist industry pulling carts and caravans, in the competition arena pulling carriages — sometimes just one horse, sometimes two, or three, or four, or six — herding cattle or rounding up wild Mustangs, drawing brewery drays through the centre of cities, or competing with fierce determination in the competition arena, the whole world over.

As Ronald Duncan also says of the horse in his poem:

All our history is his industry.
We are his heirs.
He is our inheritance.

Sport

Sport

As an athlete, the horse is beyond compare. His great strength and stamina enable him to gallop and jump with ease, his eagerness to learn allows him to perform in the dressage arena, and his willingness to please make him strain with every muscle to clear any obstacle, no matter how high, he may find in his path.

On the racetrack, the horse's inherent desire to be first will see him fight to get his head in front, and in National Hunt racing, he will throw his heart over the fences — such as formidable Chair or Becher's Brook in Liverpool, England's world-renowed Grand National — before he follows it.

Perhaps no other equestrian discipline asks for more of its participants than three-day eventing, the ultimate test of horse and man.

The combination of dressage, speed and endurance, and show jumping is based on military manouevers. Its

purpose was to test the precision, elegance, and obedience of the Army horse on the parade ground — the dressage phase; his stamina and bravery in battle — the steeplechase, roads and tracks, and cross-country, and finally his fitness after the previous phases — the show jumping.

Originally, only Army officers on military chargers were allowed to compete in the sport, but by 1924, at the Paris Olympics, three-day eventing was open to civilians as well.

The dressage test, which comprises several different movements, serves to develop harmony in the horse's physique and ability to carry out the movements while remaining calm, supple, and flexible. Each movement is marked out of 10, and the judges also give marks for the horse's paces, impulsion, and submission, as well the rider's skill at getting the best out of his horse, and his own ability.

Sport

The cross-country phases are designed to illustrate the speed, endurance, and jumping ability and accuracy — over a variety of "natural" obstacles, including water — of the horse in peak condition, as well as the rider's knowledge of his horse's fitness, his strengths and weaknesses. The cross-country phase is timed, and penalties are given for being too fast — overstretching the horse — as well as being too slow.

The final phase, show jumping, demonstrates that the horse can remain fit and sound, and able to "come back" to the rider's control after the comparative freedom of the speed and endurance phases. The show jumping tracks are usually twisting and tricky, rather than particularly big, testing the horse's suppleness and his obedience to his rider.

Because the competition is split — with dressage on the first, speed and endurance on the second, and show jumping on the third, the English called it "three-day eventing".

It became equally popular in America, where it was known as combined training, and in France it was called "concours complete d'equitation", or the "complete equestrian competition".

But in whichever country — and the sport is popular almost worldwide — the object of the competition is to "show the rider's spirit, boldness, and perfect knowledge of his horse's paces and their use across country, and to show the condition, handiness, courage, jumping ability, stamina, and speed of the well-trained horse". It is one of the very few Olympic sports in which men and women compete on equal terms.

Three-day eventing remains an Olympic sport, but in order to keep it so, a "short-format" was adopted in 2005, in which the steeplechase

Sport

and roads and tracks phases were abandoned, leaving only dressage, cross-country, and show jumping.

This has had mixed response, but the thought of the ultimate test of horse and rider being left out of future Olympic Games must surely make this compromise worthwhile.

Pure dressage and show jumping are both Olympic sports in their own right, and, like three-day eventing, include both team and individual competitions. To see a world-class horse and rider combination producing a flawless dressage test is to witness almost an equine ballet, but the power of the show jumper is no less spectacular.

Many event horses have honed their skills in the hunting field, and it is known that hunting keeps horses "sweet". Most of them adore it. They love the hounds, the sound of the horn, and most of all the adrenalin rush of galloping flat out across country, taking fences as they come.

Hunting in England has an ancient history, many of her Royal Forests being once the hunting grounds of her Kings and Queens. Legislation was controversially introduced in February 2005, banning hunting of live quarry — although bizarrely not including in that description rabbit nor rat — but those who love the sport, and the hounds and the fox, have vowed to keep going within the law to preserve it for future generations.

Hunting is also popular in North America — indeed, during the fight to resist a ban in England, American hunters were generous in their support, crossing the Atlantic specifically to attend marches and rallies. As well as fox, American packs also hunt coyote, a worthy and wily quarry. Many American packs of hounds are based on English bloodlines, and the US has returned the

Sport

favor, sending her hounds as "draft" to English packs to breed the very best — for "nose", scenting ability; "voice", their cry; speed and soundness, and for that elusive and innate ability that makes them great hunters, fox sense.

Foxhunting was famously banned by Hitler in Germany, but remains popular in other European countries, such as France, where they also hunt deer and wild boar.

The horse's great survival instinct is based on a "flight or fight" mechanism; an essentially harmless creature, he will only fight if there is no other option. He is also a herd animal, and it is this herding instinct that makes him such a glorious sight on the racecourse. It is built in him to make him want to get his nose in front — in a race he will strive with every fibre of his being to win. First is best, the strongest, the supreme.

Whether it is in England's racing "HQ", Newmarket; America's Thoroughbred heartland, Kentucky; the Melbourne Cup, for which the whole of Australia grinds to a halt, or the moneyed splendor of Dubai — home of the world's richest horserace, the US$6,000,000 Dubai World Cup — horseracing has captured the imagination worldwide and is today a multi-billion dollar industry.

The scent of money hangs over the polo field, too, wafting upwards from the steaming bodies of the lithe little "ponies", echoing from the hospitality tents, and reflected in the mirrored sunglasses of the rich and famous, who have adopted this fast and powerful equine sport as their own.

The game of polo — a sort of hockey on horseback — is thought to be around 2,000 years old, having started in China and Persia. Its name is said to be derived from "pholo", from the Tibetan word for "ball" or

Sport

"ballgame". It was established in India by the Emperor Babur, and the English teaplanters discovered the game in Manipor on the Burmese border in the 1850s, and adopted it with alacrity. The world's oldest existing polo club is the Calcutta Club, founded in 1862.

More than 77 countries now play polo. It was an Olympic sport from 1900 to 1939 and was recognized again by the International Olympic Committee in 1998. It is, however, only played professionally in a handful of countries, notably the United States, Argentina, England, and India.

Although they are called "ponies", the equines used for polo are small horses, which combine the intelligence of the Arabian, the speed of the Thoroughbred, and the agility of the Quarter Horse, although the most prized are the Argentine cross of Thoroughbred with tough little native Criollo. They usually stand only about 15 hands high, and possess that one trait that every athlete, be he human or equine, needs above all others — he has heart.

Agility is also needed in that most American of sports, the rodeo. And not just on behalf of the horse — the Bronco rider must be able to twist and turn with every movement of his fiery mount, who tries his utmost to dislodge him. The Bronco rider requires the balance of a gymnast, the timing of a springboard diver, and the grace of a dancer. He has only a thick rein attached to the horse's headcollar and the saddle to hang on to. Or he may be riding bareback, in which case he will have only a "rigging", a handhold made of leather and rawhide that is secured to the horse with a cinch with which to keep hold.

Other Western riding sports include calf roping, and reining. Like all Western competitions, reining began on the ranch; Cowboys who had to herd cattle, rope calves, and ride long distances needed reliable, agile, and obedient horses. Reining as been called the "dressage of Western riding", and, done well, it is a breathtaking balletic display of trust and obedience between horse and man.

USEFUL
INFORMATION

Useful Information

Akhal-Teke
www.akhal-teke.org

Andalusian
www.ialha.org
www.andalusian.com

Arabian
www.arabianhorses.org
www.ahtimes.com
www.waho.org
www.arabianlines.com
www.arabhorsesoc-uk.com

Appaloosa
www.appaloosa.com
www.appaloosa-horses.org
www.foundationapp.org

Brumby
www.savethebrumbies.org
www.brumbywatchaustralia.com

Camargue
www.camarguehorse.com

Chincoteague
www.chincoteague.com
www.pony-chincoteague.com
www.mistyofchincoteague.org

Cleveland Bay
www.clevelandbay.com
www.clevelandbay.org
www.rbst.org.uk (Rare Breeds Survival Trust)

Dartmoor Pony
www.dartmoorponysociety.com
www.dartmoorpony.com
www.rbst.org.uk

Dutch Warmblood
www.kwpn.nl
www.nawpn.org

Exmoor Pony
www.exmoorponysociety.org.uk
www.rbst.org.uk

Falabella
www.falabellahorse.com
www.falabellafmha.com
www.falabella.co.uk
www.falabellabreeders.org

Florida Cracker
fcha.flahorse.com
www.gaitedhorses.net

Friesian
www.friesianhorsesociety.com
www.fhana.com

Haflinger
www.haflingerhorse.com
www.haflinger.net
www.haflinger.ca

Hanoverian
www.hanoverian.org
www.hanoverian-gb.org.uk
www.hanoverian.com

Useful Information

Highland Pony
www.highlandponysociety.com
www.highlandponyenthusiasts.co.uk

Holsteiner
www.holsteiner.com

Icelandic Horse
www.icelandics.org
www.icelandichorse.is
www.icelandicsonice.com
www.gaitedhorses.net

Irish Draught
www.irishdraught.com
www.irishdraught.ie

Lipizzaner
www.uslr.org
www.lipizzan.org
www.lipizzaner.co.uk
www.lipizzaner.org.uk

Lusitano
www.ialha.org
www.andalusian.com
www.lusobreedsociety.co.uk
www.bapsh.co.uk
www.bapshweb.co.uk

Missouri Fox Trotter
www.mfthba.com
www.gaitedhorses.net

Morgan
www.morganhorse.com
www.morgan-horses.org
www.morganhorse.ca
www.morganmuseum.org
www.morganhorse.org.uk

Mustang
www.wildhorseandburro.blm.gov
www.mustang-horses.org

National Show Horse
www.nshregistry.org
www.gaitedhorses.net

Norwegian Fjord
www.nfhr.com
www.fjord-horse.co.uk

Oldenburg
www.isroldenburg.org
www.oldenburghorse.com
www.oldenburghorses.com

Paint
www.abha.com
www.aphaonline.com

Quarter Horse
www.aqha.com
www.cqha.ca

Palomino
www.palominohba.com
www.palominohorseassoc.com
www.britishpalominosociety.co.uk

Useful Information

Paso Fino
www.pfha.org
www.pasofinos.com
www.gaitedhorses.net

Peruvian Paso
www.pphrna.org
www.gaitedhorses.net

Pony of the Americas
www.poac.org

Przewalski (Asiatic Wild Horse)
www.treemail.nl/takh

Rocky Mountain Horse
www.rmhorse.com
www.gaitedhorses.net

Saddlebred
www.asha.net
www.american-saddlebred.com
www.gaitedhorses.net

Selle Francais
www.sellefrancais.org
www.sellefrancais.fr/HTML_GB

Shetland Pony
www.shetlandponystudbooksociety.co.uk
www.shetlandminiature.com

Shire
www.shirehorse.org
www.shire-horse.org.uk
www.canadianshirehorse.com

Thoroughbred
www.jockeyclub.com
www.thejockeyclub.co.uk

Trakehner
www.americantrakehner.com
www.trakehners-international.com
www.cantrak.on.ca

Welsh Ponies & Cobs
www.welshpony.org
www.wpcs.uk.com

Breed Index